The Wildfowler's World

The Wildfowler's World

Pictures by Hanson Carroll
Text by Nelson Bryant

Foreword by Jack Samson

WINCHESTER PRESS

ACKNOWLEDGMENT

Grateful acknowledgment must be made to the editors who bravely assigned some of the photographs in this book as editorial illustrations for stories in their magazines, knowing full well the limitations of weather and the unpredictability of waterfowl.

Some of the results from these assignments which are printed here have previously appeared in *American Sportsman, Field & Stream, Outdoor Life, Sports Afield, Sports Illustrated,* and *Vermont Life.*

Copyright © 1973 by Hanson Carroll
All rights reserved
Library of Congress Catalog Card Number 73-78818
ISBN 0-87691-107-6
Published by Winchester Press
460 Park Avenue, New York 10022
Printed in the United States of America

To all the waterfowling widows of the world,
hunting companions past and present,
Ducks Unlimited, loyal retrievers,
and makers of good bourbon and fine shotguns.

FOREWORD

From the combination of Hanson Carroll's remarkable photographs and the evocative prose of Nelson Bryant has evolved a book to gladden the heart and stir the memory of every waterfowler. Carroll, a Vermonter, and Bryant, a native of Martha's Vineyard, have come by their love and knowledge of the sport almost as second nature, and both the pictures and the text reflect a lifetime spent in blind, pit and pass, from the wind-scarred dunes of Cape Cod to the black mud marshes of Barnegat and the sandy surf of Cape Hatteras.

The pictures in this splendid book, drawn from the best photographs taken during nearly two decades of wildfowling, have recorded its beauty and drama in many varied aspects of season, time and weather, and much of its magic has never been better communicated on film. There are, of course, other aspects of wildfowling that defy capture on film, even for an artist like Hans Carroll—for what duckhunter hasn't experienced the sudden agony of a hipboot full of icewater, the sudden blush that comes from making a perfect "shot" with your safety on, the sudden tumult of getting a lapful of hot coffee and wet Lab puppy at the same time? No doubt the authors knew that fellow duckhunters would inject these things for themselves as they turned the pages, anyway.

All in all, *The Wildfowler's World* has succeeded in revealing more than I would have thought possible of the intangible essence of the sport it concerns. And on those out-of-season days when I can almost taste my hunger to get back on the marsh, into a blind or duck boat, I'm sure that revisiting this fine book will ease the pain, at least a little.

—Jack Samson

Contents

PREFACE
11

Dawn
14

Flight
28

Decoys
46

The Hunt
54

Blind, Boat and Sinkbox
68

Man and Dog
78

The Urge to Retrieve
90

Dusk
110

PREFACE

Although each might deny it, duck hunters and poets have a common hunger: both seek solace, inspiration, and joy in the natural world.

But with few exceptions, modern poets have not found hunting to their liking, and their observations on waterfowling traditionally run the course from William Cullen Bryant's "vainly the fowler's eye might mark thy flight to do thee wrong," to Ogden Nash's comment that a "grown-up man with pluck and luck is hoping to outwit a duck."

Yet the duck hunter's world embraces the raw goods of poetry: surf moaning on the outer beach, black ducks hurtling skyward from a mountaintop pond; Canada geese measuring the night with great strokes of their powerful wings; whistlers a thousand feet high glinting in the upward-slanting light of a sun that is no longer visible to land-bound creatures; scoters black as tar buckets on a stormy bay, wearing patches as white as the broken waves.

And there is the aroma of strong coffee rising from a thermos cup held in cramped, numbed fingers, or the musty odor of a retriever's coat as he sleeps close to the hearth, or the explosive warmth of a fireplace and good bourbon at the end of a day's hunt.

Poets or not, waterfowlers endeavor for a tiny portion of their days to capture something of their prehistory, something of a time when there were no barriers between man and the world of wind and wings, sky and sea.

The Wildfowler's World

Dawn

Dawn is a duck hunter's dearest hour. He might, indeed, be said to measure his life by the number of dawns he has spent in quest of waterfowl on inland or salt marshes, on ocean beaches, or crouched, shivering, in a blind on one of the magnificent, seemingly endless sounds and bays behind North Carolina's barrier beaches.

Dawn has become doubly important to the waterfowler now that the law does not allow him to shoot after sunset, for the birds tend to fly at the day's start and end. Dawn is promise, a time of sweet anticipation. And no matter how weary a man might be, or how little sleep he had the night before, the exquisite excitement of watching daylight arrive, whether it comes in a splendid rush of color or creeps onstage in muted grays, never wanes. And all discomforts—fingers numbed by setting out decoys, or legs trembling from a long tramp in waders through rich-smelling muck, or a face stung by bitterly cold, wind-driven spray—are as nothing.

Dawn is a beginning, and the waterfowler huddled in the aching dampness of a sinkbox, or in the hollow of a sand dune on Cape Cod, or in willows or rushes beside the great Missouri, greets it, like a lover, with both arms. The world is asleep, but he is abroad and overhead he can hear the whispered rush of wind through wings.

Racing the rising sun, waterfowlers set their decoys, for soon the birds will be flying. Arrangement of the blocks may be a matter of art, science or accident, depending on the hunter.

Often the setting out of decoys is shrouded by morning mists.

The naturalness of the spread is enhanced by using decoys in different attitudes.

Not snow nor ice, not numbed fingers nor snarled anchor lines can weaken the duckhunter's dedication.

Blocks set at last, it only remains for the wildfowlers to move into their blinds and savor the last silence of the marsh as they wait for the birds to start flying.

Flight From the swift, powerful, direct flight of the black duck to the equally swift but erratic flight of the teals or scaup, each species of waterfowl has its unique way of moving through the skies.

The alert duck hunter is mindful of this, for most of the time he will see the birds at a distance too great to pick out individual markings. Any hunter worth his salt should be able to distinguish between the birds on which the season is open or closed, and he must know them in their winter plumage, must know their size, their appearance in silhouette and whether they leap directly from the water before taking wing, as do the puddle ducks, or run along the water, in the manner of diving ducks.

It is not, as a practical matter, necessary that a hunter be able to identify all of the forty-odd species of ducks, geese and swans regularly found within the continental United States: he would do better to concentrate on those commonly seen in the area he hunts, realizing that as the shooting season moves along, some of the early-arriving species will leave and latecomers will take their place.

Some birds cannot be mistaken for any other species. The Canada goose circling, calling and descending to join his clamoring brethren in a Maryland cornfield is, for example, alone in his magnificence, and, although less dramatic, black, heavy-bodied scoters beating their way low over the gray, heaving ocean are equally unique.

With the advent of dawn, from a thousand resting places the birds take wing, sometimes singly . . .

...*sometimes in small flights of two or three*...

... and sometimes in deafeningly larger flights that almost defy estimation.

Canada geese, like these laboring above the surf at Cape Hatteras, are prolific indeed, breeding in most of Canada and wintering in most of the United States.

In contrast, the greater snow goose breeds in the Arctic coast and winters only in a small stretch of Maryland–North Carolina coast.

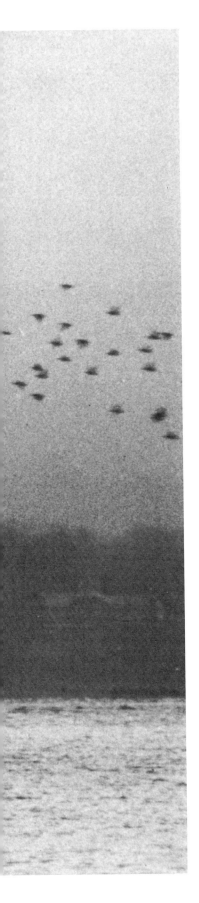

With birds in the air, many hunters enhance the visual appeal of their decoys by calling, hoping to invite the closer inspection of their spread that will afford a shot.

Decoys

There was once a boy of eleven, nearly forty years ago, who crept stealthily to the shore of a salt pond with his first shotgun and delivered a charge of No. 6 shot into three black ducks he saw sitting on the water.

The roar of rage that came from an unseen blind sent him racing home in terror through the scrub oaks. He had unwittingly peppered the decoys of an old duck hunter known to have a fierce temper.

From that time on the boy never shot birds on the water unless they were cripples, and he also began to acquire some decoys of his own, reasoning that if he could be fooled so could a duck.

More than a half-century has passed since the era of waterfowl market hunting in the United States ended, but during that unprecedented slaughter of ducks, geese, swans and shorebirds the folk art of decoy carving, a pursuit that has a growing roster of devotees, was born.

Every region from New England to the Mississippi had its carvers of distinction. The best work of these men was characterized by a startling purity of line and concept. And, equally important, their decoys functioned. They resembled their live counterparts and behaved like them on the water.

Today, plastics, rubber and other materials are used to mass-produce gunning, as opposed to decorative, decoys, although some are still made of wood and cork.

Some waterfowl are satisfied by the crudest representations of themselves. Scoters will decoy to Clorox bottles painted black, and blue geese at James Bay will swing to clumps of mud topped with a stick and a white feather or rag. Other species—and the black duck is among the wariest—will shy away if anything looks wrong; if, as an example, the decoys glint in the sun.

46

The decoy's shape, aided by a touch of color, is the essence of the duplicity, along with the way the counterfeit rides both rough and smooth water.

The final criterion of how well blocks have been set is how they look to the ducks, and the final tribute comes in the form of wings set for landing.

Luckily, waterfowl are not especially sensitive
to subtleties of coloring and marking . . .

. . . for no decoy could ever match the exquisite texture and iridescent markings of the real bird.

The Hunt

One could be huddled on the bare, dark rocks of the Thimble Islands off Connecticut in Long Island Sound as a December wind cuts deep, waiting for scaup to come to the 75 or 100 decoys one has set out at dawn . . .

One could be flat on his back in a scull boat off Maine's forbidding snow-spattered coast . . .

One could be crouched in a wild-rose thicket on Martha's Vineyard as a northeast gale whirls stinging sand along the beach and usually wary black ducks, harried to distraction by the wind, come without caution to a handful of decoys . . .

One could be in the mangrove jungles of the Yucatan as teal come hurtling by . . . or in a Kansas cornfield . . . or on a backwater of the Mississippi or the Missouri, or in Arkansas' flooded pin oaks or rice fields . . . or on the desolate shores of James Bay where the tide comes in almost as fast as a man can walk . . . or on one of the storied Eastern coastal bays or sounds—the Chesapeake, Currituck, Albemarle, Pamlico.

Beside the sea or away from it, whether by lake, bay, pond, river or inland marsh, one hides, or remains motionless, and waits, sometimes using decoys, sometimes, if one has the skill, calling the wild birds down from the sky. Whatever the place, the magic is the same, and for a little while man forgets his mundane duties and enters the primitive world of the hunter, responding to an urge that is as valid as the desire to love a woman or beget a child.

First shots are often taken when the sun has barely peeked over the horizon.

Many hunters consider wildfowling the shotgunner's ultimate test...

. . . for wing shots come at all angles, speeds and ranges.

Flying spray will quickly show the gunner what he did wrong.

Hit and marked, a whistler plummets into the water.

Inland waterfowlers often have good shooting by hiding in the bushes and grass on the edge of some small upland pond . . .

. . . or from goose blinds on cut-over grain fields in New England, or cornfield pit blinds in Maryland.

Dark against an exploding wave, a lone bird flashes past a pair of seacoast gunners.

Blind, Boat and Sinkbox All

successful duck hunters must learn to hide from the ever-searching and incredibly keen eyes of the birds they seek to shoot. The duck hunter must wear drab or camouflaged clothing, and he must remember to keep his face hidden as much as possible and to follow the birds with his eyes rather than abrupt turnings of his head, for sudden movement is readily spotted by ducks and geese. There are even some waterfowlers who slop green and brown paint over their shotguns, but this is an unwarranted excess.

Concealment can take many forms. Nearly forty years ago, I had one of the best shots of my life on a salt marsh by merely standing upright and motionless for an hour until I was plastered with falling snow. During the latter part of my vigil, goldeneyes pitched into the open water at my feet until there were a hundred or more in an area of less than half an acre. I shall not tell how many birds fell when I put them to flight and fired, because I did not, in those days, realize the importance of bag limits, but my family wearied of eating goldeneyes during the next two weeks.

Such rudimentary hiding, whether kneeling in bushes or grass or hunkering under the twisted branches of a wind-tortured pitch pine, is enough in certain situations, especially flight shooting, but when one intends to decoy ducks, some form of blind is essential. It may be no more than a hole hacked out of the center of a clump of wild rose bushes along the seacoast, or it may be an elaborate, roofed-over shelter covered with marsh grass and complete with warming stove and coffee pot. It may be a pit blind in Maryland with a metal top that is swung out of the way when the birds fly within range, or it may be a reed-covered blind mounted on stakes in open water, as in Currituck Sound.

One of the most efficient blinds, now outlawed, was the floating sinkbox in which, anchored and surrounded by decoys, the gunner lay flat on his back with most of his body below water level. Variations of these blinds are still used. In North Carolina, for example, one finds concrete boxes (like the one pictured at right) far out in a shallow bay or sound, surrounded by a floating wood and canvas apron that rises and falls with the tide.

Both migration and feeding routes often follow the course of rivers, and floating blinds like this St. Lawrence rig are eminently practical.

Wearing the muted colors of the marsh, hunters on smaller rivers can stalk and jump-shoot their birds by canoe.

A herring gull figurehead on the sneak box can act as a "confidence" decoy to persuade ducks that there is no danger.

Having worked up close to a dozen black ducks, hunters rise to shoot. At right, scull-boat gunners retrieve a long-tailed old-squaw.

Man and Dog

He may be called Sam or Bo or Jim, with an ancestry as mixed as your own, or he may have a complicated title and an irreproachable bloodline that traces directly back to champion retrievers, but, more than anything else, and whether his performance in the field is mediocre or brilliant, he is your friend.

Whether mutt, or Brittany, Labrador, Golden or Chesapeake, he was your friend when he was a foolish pup trying to understand the meaning of such commands as "stay," "heel," "fetch," "mark" and "give." He was still your friend when, a year later, he could not contain his eagerness when he saw his first birds coming to the decoys and had to be whacked to be kept from moving. He was your friend on still, foggy dawns when you could hear a door slam across a mile of bay and the ducks were ghostly wraiths in the murk. He was beside you in the blind when he was no longer young, shivering, sometimes pushing against you for warmth, his coat matted with ice and falling snow, but he was always intense, his eyes searching the skies for faraway birds. That was the winter when, lame from age and countless hours in the cold and wet, he ignored your warning and swam a half-mile out into the choppy waters of the bay to retrieve a duck you had winged.

You were a young man when you bought him. Twelve years later when he died you were barely middle-aged, and in your sadness on that day you thought it unreasonable that man and dog could not share an equal span of seasons. But later you learned that the memory of his devotion would fill all your years and that there could be room in your heart for another friend.

For many wildfowlers, dog work is the real challenge and much of the delight of duck hunting. The well-trained retriever is staunch to shot, but readily takes a line . . .

...*never shirks water, no matter how frigid*...

. . . tenaciously pursues cripples—below the water, too, in the case of diving ducks—and tenderly delivers the bird to its master's hand.

A good shake is the inevitable consequence of a cold swim, as well as a constant hazard to the forgetful duckhunter.

Heeling is a simpler accomplishment, and a natural one for a true companion in sport.

The Urge to Retrieve In the best
duck dogs, the urge to retrieve is a passion.

Last winter a North Carolina duck-hunting guide revealed to a sportsman who admired the efficiency and dedication of his Chesapeake Bay retriever that the training of the animal had been a simple matter.

"I take a new dog hunting for a week. If he does the job, or shows that he could do it given a little more time, I keep him. If he doesn't, I give him away and get another."

This simplistic approach to training is not altogether farfetched, for if a dog lacks the urge to retrieve, there is small chance that he will ever be good at it. He can be forced into the role, but he will lack verve and tenacity.

A good retriever, whether honed to a fine edge at home or in field trials, enters each hunt with fierce joy. He loves his job and the man who leads him to it. Each downed bird is a challenge, and his pride can scarcely allow him to fail; he must bring it back.

Etched in every hunter's heart is the grace and glory of his dog's stylish retrieves: the hurdling lunge from bank to water . . .

. . . and the joyous return with head and tail high and sunlight gleaming on wet flanks.

Churning through the marsh, a disciplined Lab stops short at whistle and awaits his orders.

Wildfowling happens in the most varied of locales, from the desolate tidal flats of James Bay...

... *to the beaver ponds of the Northeast; but whatever the situation, a good retriever is an invaluable partner.*

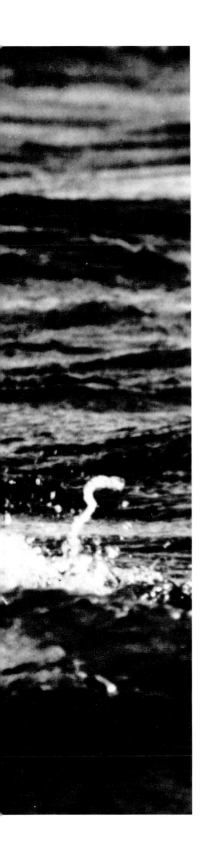

Retrieving sea ducks is probably the most arduous retrieving of all. Drenched by spray, this hunter strives to aid his tide-battered retriever.

Retrieving a limit of sea ducks can even transform rocks into a welcome resting place by the end of day.

Dusk

Before the days of the federal curfew that stops waterfowling at sunset, a great many birds were taken as the last light faded.

Black ducks, as a case in point, usually begin to move into sheltered coves and ponds from open water just before it is too dark to see them, and many hunters enjoy lingering, gun empty, in some secluded marsh to watch this evening flight. In Eastern coastal areas, the blacks will be preceded by croaking black-crowned night herons and sharp-eyed herring gulls.

When the day is stormy or overcast, and the light begins to fail before the sun has gone down, the ducks often begin to fly a little ahead of schedule. At such times, the waterfowler would do well to remain alert until the last minute, for he may have good shooting just as sky and water merge into a single gray and a muskrat leaves his domed house in the marsh to cut a wide furrow in the darkening water.

As light fails, the harsh images and sounds of day recede, and waterfowl seek their nighttime resting places.

Often, in that breathless twilight, the wildfowler has a few final minutes before the sunset curfew to take his final bird.

Then the last rays of the sun have vanished, and man and dog can cast thoughts back to thrills of the day in the quiet satisfaction of dusk.

Finally, most wildfowl are safely resting in their nighttime sanctuaries, and no sound of man interrupts the muted chuckling of ducks at rest.

Silent sharers of a magical time, man and dog trudge home, the day's hunt done.